FROGS
RANAS

By Sindy McKay

Translated by Lingorama

TREASURE BAY

Parent's Introduction

Whether your child is a beginning, reluctant, or eager reader, this book offers a fun and easy way to support your child in reading.

Developed with reading education specialists, We Both Read books invite you and your child to take turns reading aloud. You read the left-hand pages of the book, and your child reads the right-hand pages—which have been written at one of six early reading levels. The result is a wonderful new reading experience and faster reading development!

I like taking turns!

Me too!

This is a special bilingual edition of a We Both Read book. On each page the text is in two languages. This offers the opportunity for you and your child to read in either language. It also offers the opportunity to learn new words in another language.

In some books, a few challenging words are introduced in the parent's text with **bold** lettering. Pointing out and discussing these words can help to build your child's reading vocabulary. If your child is a beginning reader, it may be helpful to run a finger under the text as each of you reads. Please also notice that a "talking parent" icon ⟨⟩ precedes the parent's text, and a "talking child" icon ⟨⟩ precedes the child's text.

If your child struggles with a word, you can encourage "sounding it out," but not all words can be sounded out. Your child might pick up clues about a difficult word from other words in the sentence or a picture on the page. If your child struggles with a word for more than five seconds, it is usually best to simply say the word.

As you read together, praise your child's efforts and keep the reading fun. Simply sharing the enjoyment of reading together will increase your child's skills and help to start your child on a lifetime of reading enjoyment!

Introducción a los padres

No importa que su hijo sea un lector principiante, reacio o ansioso, este libro le ofrece una manera fácil y divertida de ayudarlo en la lectura.

Desarrollado con especialistas en educación de lectura, los libros We Both Read lo invitan a usted y a su hijo a turnarse para leer en voz alta. Usted lee las páginas de la izquierda del libro y su hijo lee las páginas de la derecha, que se han escrito en uno de los seis primeros niveles de lectura. ¡El resultado es una nueva y maravillosa experiencia de lectura y un desarrollo más rápido de la misma!

Esta es una edición especial bilingüe de un libro de We Both Read. En cada página el texto aparece en dos idiomas. Esto le ofrece la oportunidad de que usted y su hijo lean en cualquiera de los dos idiomas. También le ofrece la oportunidad de aprender nuevas palabras en otro idioma.

En algunos libros, se presentan en el texto de los padres algunas palabras difíciles con letras **en negrita**. Señalar y discutir estas palabras puede ayudar a desarrollar el vocabulario de lectura de su hijo. Si su hijo es un lector principiante, puede ser útil deslizar un dedo debajo del texto a medida que cada uno de ustedes lea. Tenga en cuenta también que un ícono de "padre que habla" ⊙ precede al texto del padre y un ícono de "niño que habla" ⊙ precede al texto del niño.

Si su hijo tiene dificultad con una palabra, puede animarlo a "pronunciarla", pero no todas las palabras se pueden pronunciar fácilmente. Su hijo puede obtener pistas sobre una palabra difícil a partir de otras palabras en la oración o de una imagen en la página. Si su hijo tiene dificultades con una palabra durante más de cinco segundos, por lo general es mejor decir simplemente la palabra.

Mientras leen juntos, elogie los esfuerzos de su hijo y mantenga la diversión de la lectura. ¡El simple hecho de compartir el placer de leer juntos aumentará las destrezas de su hijo y lo ayudará a que disfrute de la lectura para toda la vida!

Frogs • *Ranas*

A We Both Read Book • *Un libro de la serie We Both Read*
Level K-1 • *Nivel K–1*
Guided Reading: Level C • *Lectura guiada: Nivel C*

With special thanks to
Erica Ely, M.S.,
Curatorial Assistant for Herpetology at the California Academy of
Sciences, for her review and advice on the material in this book.

Queremos agradecer especialmente a
Erica Ely, M.S.,
Asistente curatorial de herpetología en la Academia de Ciencias de
California, por su revisión y consejo sobre el material de este libro.

Use of photographs provided by iStock, Shutterstock, and Dreamstime.

We Both Read® is a registered trademark of Treasure Bay, Inc.

Published by Treasure Bay, Inc.
P.O. Box 119
Novato, CA 94948 USA

Printed in Malaysia

Library of Congress Catalog Card Number: 2020941826

ISBN: 978-1-60115-114-8

Visit us online at WeBothRead.com

PR-11-20

TABLE OF CONTENTS
ÍNDICE

Wallace's flying tree frog
Rana voladora de Wallace

Ribbit! Ribbit! Frogs are everywhere. They are amphibians (am-FIH-bee-inz), so their bodies are the same temperature as the air or water around them. They live on every continent except Antarctica. That continent is too cold!

◆

¡Croac, croac! Las ranas están en todos lados. Son anfibias, por eso su cuerpo tiene la misma temperatura que el aire o el agua que las rodea. Viven en todos los continentes excepto la Antártida. ¡Ese continente es demasiado frío!

Wallace's flying tree frog
Rana voladora de Wallace

Frogs can be green.
Frogs can be red.

———◆———

Las ranas pueden ser verdes.
Las ranas pueden ser rojas.

Red poison dart frog
Rana flecha roja

The smallest known frog
La rana más pequeña que se conoce

Frogs come in many different colors, patterns, and sizes. The **smallest** known frog is less than a half inch long. The largest is the goliath frog, which can be as **big** as a **small** dog! Another very **big** frog is the African bullfrog.

◆

*Hay ranas de muchos colores, formas y tamaños diferentes. La rana más **pequeña** que se conoce mide menos de media pulgada de largo. La más **grande** se llama rana Goliat, ¡y puede ser tan **grande** como un perro **pequeño**! Otra rana muy **grande** es la rana toro africana.*

4

African bullfrog
(actual size)

*Rana toro africana
(tamaño real)*

The smallest known frog
(actual size)

*La rana más pequeña que se conoce
(tamaño real)*

Frogs can be **big**.
Frogs can be **small**.

*Las ranas pueden ser **grandes**.*
*Las ranas pueden ser **pequeñas**.*

The skin of a frog is very distinctive. It feels slimy and moist. Frogs breathe through their skin. When they **need** a drink, they take in **water** through their skin.

———————◆———————

*La piel de la rana es muy particular. Se siente viscosa y húmeda. Las ranas respiran a través de la piel. Cuando **necesitan** beber, toman **agua** a través de la piel.*

Frogs **need water.**

Las ranas **necesitan agua.**

Wood frog
Rana de bosque

Frogs' eyes bulge out from the sides of their heads. This lets them **see** in almost every direction. They **hear** with ears that usually can't be **seen**.

♦

*Los ojos de las ranas sobresalen a los lados de la cabeza. Esto les permite **ver** en casi todas las direcciones. Para **oír** usan oídos que casi nunca se **ven**.*

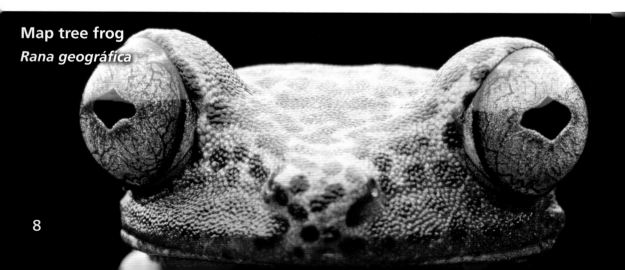

Map tree frog
Rana geográfica

Ear
Oído

Eastern frog
Rana oriental

Frogs can **see** well.
Frogs can **hear** well.

◆

Las ranas pueden **ver** bien.
Las ranas pueden **oír** bien.

Ear
Oído

Green tree frog
Rana verde

Most frogs have long, sticky tongues that are used to grab something to **eat**. They flick their tongue out and wrap it around a bug. The tongue then snaps back and throws the bug down the frog's throat.

◆

Muchas ranas tienen lenguas largas y pegajosas que usan para atrapar lo que *comen*. Sacan la lengua y la envuelven alrededor de un insecto. Después, la lengua se retrae muy rápido y arroja al insecto dentro de la garganta de la rana.

10

 **Most** frogs **eat** bugs.

———◆———

Muchas ranas ***comen*** *insectos.*

Green marsh frog
Rana europea común

Frogs make a variety of noises—especially at night. Many frogs have throat sacs beneath their mouth that swell to make the sounds even louder!

Some frogs croak.

———◆———

Las ranas hacen una variedad de ruidos, especialmente de noche. ¡Muchas ranas tienen sacos vocales debajo de la boca que se hinchan para hacer los sonidos aún más fuertes!

Algunas *ranas croan.*

Green marsh frog
Rana europea común

Painted reed frog
Rana de lámina veteada

Some frogs click.
Some frogs grunt.

◆

Algunas ranas chasquean.
Algunas ranas gruñen.

European tree frog
Ranita de San Antonio

Green marsh frog
Rana europea común

African clawed frog
Rana africana de uñas

Frogs have webbed feet for swimming **fast**. They have very powerful back legs for jumping. Some people have contests to see how **far** their frog can jump!

◆

*La ranas tienen patas palmeadas para nadar **rápido**. Tienen patas traseras muy potentes para saltar. ¡Algunas personas hacen concursos para ver lo **lejos** que puede saltar su rana!*

14

 Frogs can jump **far**.
Frogs can swim **fast**.

———◆———

*Las ranas pueden saltar **lejos**.*
*Las ranas pueden nadar **rápido**.*

15

Wallace's flying tree frog
Rana voladora de Wallace

Almost all frogs can jump and swim. Their webbed feet help them to swim. Using long, strong back legs, many frogs can leap great distances. Many tree frogs use their webbed feet to help them soar and glide from tree to tree.

————◆————

Casi todas las ranas pueden saltar y nadar. Las patas palmeadas les ayudan a nadar. Muchas ranas pueden saltar grandes distancias usando las patas traseras, largas y fuertes. Muchas ranas arborícolas usan las patas palmeadas para ayudarlas a elevarse y deslizarse de árbol en árbol.

Dumpy frog diving
Una rana arborícola se zambulle

 Some frogs can **almost** fly!

¡Algunas ranas **casi** pueden volar!

17

Adult frog with recently laid eggs
Rana adulta con huevos recién puestos

Tomato frog eggs
Huevos de rana tomate

Almost all frogs start out life as an egg. Most eggs are laid in water. Soon the eggs hatch into **tadpoles**. Like fish, **tadpoles** have gills that let them breathe underwater. Some people think **tadpoles** look like giant **heads** with long **tails**!

◆

*Casi todas las ranas empiezan su vida como un huevo. La mayoría de los huevos se ponen en el agua. Pronto, los huevos eclosionan en **renacuajos**. Como los peces, los **renacuajos** tienen branquias que les permiten respirar bajo el agua. ¡Algunas personas piensan que los **renacuajos** parecen **cabezas** gigantes con **colas** largas!*

Tadpoles
Renacuajos

Tail
Cola

Tadpole
Renacuajo

Head
Cabeza

Tadpoles have big **heads**.
Tadpoles have big **tails**.

Los **renacuajos** tienen **cabezas** grandes.
Los renacuajos tienen **colas** grandes.

Tadpoles
Renacuajos

Masked tree froglet
Renacuajo con patas, rana arborícola enmascarada

As tadpoles grow, their tails start to disappear and their legs grow longer. **Now** they can breathe air like we do.

◆

*A medida que los renacuajos van creciendo, las colas comienzan a desaparecer y las patas crecen más largas. **Ahora** pueden respirar aire como nosotros.*

Life Cycle of a Frog

Ciclo de vida de una rana

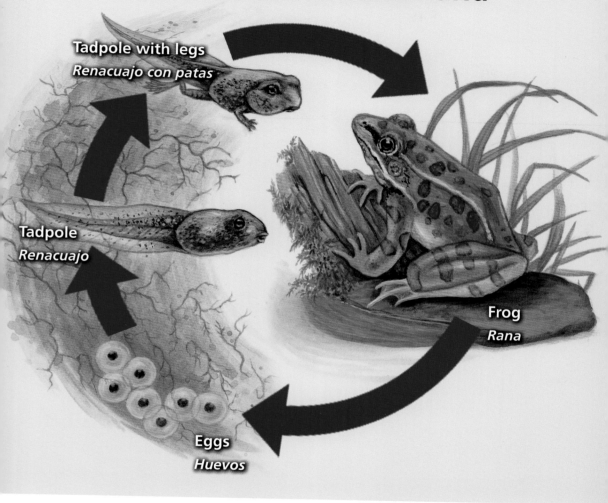

Tadpole with legs
Renacuajo con patas

Tadpole
Renacuajo

Frog
Rana

Eggs
Huevos

The tadpole is **now** a frog.

Ahora el renacuajo es una rana.

American bullfrog
Rana toro

Toads and frogs are close relatives. In many ways they are alike. In some ways they are different. Frogs live near water and have moist, slimy skin. **Toads** spend more time on land and have **dry**, bumpy skin.

◆

*Las ranas y los **sapos** son parientes cercanos. En muchos aspectos son parecidos. En otros, son diferentes. Las ranas viven cerca del agua y tienen la piel húmeda y viscosa. Los **sapos** pasan más tiempo en la tierra y tienen la piel **seca** y llena de bultos.*

Common toad
Sapo común

Frogs must be wet.
Toads can be **dry**.

Las ranas deben estar húmedas.
Los **sapos** pueden estar **secos**.

Cane toad
Sapo de caña

23

Red-eyed tree frog
Rana verde de ojos rojos

Frogs and toads are an important part of the food chain. They are both prey and predator. Many have developed ways to avoid being eaten by **snakes**, lizards, birds, or other predators. One way is to climb high into the safety of a tree.

———◆———

*Las ranas y los sapos son una parte importante de la cadena alimentaria. Son presas y depredadores. Muchos han desarrollado formas de evitar que se los coman las **serpientes**, los lagartos, los pájaros, u otros depredadores. Una forma es subir a lo alto de un árbol seguro.*

African bullfrog
Rana toro africana

Frogs eat bugs. **Snakes** eat frogs.

———◆———

Las ranas comen insectos.
*Las **serpientes** comen ranas.*

Snake hunting frog
Una serpiente caza a una rana

25

Woodhouse toad
Sapo de Woodhouse

Gray toad
Sapo gris

Another way frogs and **toads** stay safe is through camouflage (KA-muh-flahj). The skin color and pattern of the animal allows it to blend in with the environment.

———◆———

*Las ranas y los **sapos** también se mantienen a salvo a través del camuflaje. El color de la piel y el aspecto del animal le permite confundirse con el entorno.*

Vietnamese mossy frog
Rana musgo

26

Yellow-bellied toads
Sapo de vientre amarillo

Can you see the **toads**?

⸺ ◆ ⸺

*¿Puedes ver los **sapos**?*

Red strawberry poison dart frog

Rana flecha fresa

Harlequin poison dart frog

Rana arlequín venenosa

Green and black poison dart frog

Rana venenosa verdinegra

Some frogs and toads are poisonous. The poison is on their skin, so it can be dangerous to even touch them. They are usually brightly colored to warn their predators to **stay away**.

———◆———

Algunas ranas y sapos son venenosos. El veneno está en la piel, así que puede ser peligroso incluso tocarlos. Suelen ser de colores brillantes para advertir a sus depredadores: ¡Aléjate!

Three-striped poison dart frog

Rana venenosa de 3 rayas

Blue poison dart frog

Rana flecha azul

Red striped poison dart frog

Rana venenosa rojiza

Red strawberry poison dart frog

Rana flecha fresa

Dyeing dart frog

Rana de teñido

Stay away and do not eat me!

*¡**Aléjate** y no me comas!*

Yellow-banded poison dart frog
Sapito minero

Golden dart frog, which may be the most toxic frog in the world

Rana dorada venenosa, que puede ser la rana más tóxica del mundo

Some native people of the Amazon rainforest use the poison from these frogs to help them hunt. They make darts from palm leaves. The sharp end of a dart touches the skin of a frog to collect some poison. A blowgun is then used to fire the dart at the hunter's prey.

———◆———

Algunos pueblos nativos de la selva amazónica usan el veneno de estas ranas para cazar más fácilmente. Hacen dardos con hojas de palma. La punta afilada de un dardo toca la piel de una rana para recoger un poco de veneno. Luego usan una cerbatana para disparar el dardo a la presa del cazador.

The frog is not hurt.

No se lastima a la rana.

Wood frog
Rana de bosque

Water in a wood frog's body can turn into ice in the winter. When the ice melts in the spring, the frog is fine!

The dumpy tree frog is sometimes called the smiley tree frog. Can you see why?

A **glass** frog has skin on its **belly** that lets you see its internal organs!

◆

El agua en el cuerpo de una rana de bosque puede convertirse en hielo en el invierno. Cuando el hielo se derrite en la primavera, ¡la rana está perfecta!

A la rana arborícola a veces le dicen rana sonriente. ¿Puedes ver por qué?

*¡La piel de la **panza** de la rana de **cristal** te permite ver los órganos internos!*

Dumpy frog
Rana arborícola

Glass frog
Rana de cristal

The **belly** of this frog is like **glass**!

¡La **panza** de esta rana parece de **cristal**!

Panda bear tree frogs, also Amazonian milk frogs
Rana de oso panda, o rana lechera amazónica

There are so many different kinds of frogs! The panda bear tree frogs have colors similar to panda bears. The Malaysian horned frog is camouflaged to look like a dead leaf.
The Argentine horned frog has a huge mouth that is almost half the size of its body.

———————◆———————

¡Hay tantos tipos diferentes de rana! Las ranas de oso panda tienen los mismos colores que los osos panda. La rana hoja malaya se camufla para parecer una hoja muerta. El escuerzo argentino tiene una boca enorme que mide casi la mitad del tamaño de su cuerpo.

Malaysian horned frog
Rana hoja malaya

Argentine horned frog
Escuerzo argentino

It eats lots of bugs!

¡Come muchos insectos!

Frogs are an important part of a healthy environment here on Earth. They help humans by eating bugs and helping to keep ponds and rivers clean.

◆

Las ranas son una parte importante de la salud del medioambiente aquí en la Tierra. Ayudan a los humanos comiendo insectos y ayudando a mantener limpios los estanques y los ríos.

Kids like frogs.

A los niños les gustan las ranas.

37

Frog on old tire in pond

Rana sobre una llanta vieja en un estanque

Many types of frogs are in danger of dying out, and some are already gone forever. Their habitats are being destroyed to make room for roads, houses, and farms. Water pollution also destroys habitats.

◆

Muchos tipos de ranas están en peligro de extinción, y algunas ya han desaparecido para siempre. Se destruyen sus hábitats para hacer espacio para carreteras, casas y granjas. La contaminación del agua también destruye los hábitats.

Frog in polluted creek

Rana en un arroyo contaminado

This is bad for the frogs.

Esto es malo para las ranas.

Wallace's flying tree frog
Rana voladora de Wallace

It is up to all of us to make sure that frogs have clean, safe habitats where they can continue to thrive. Healthy, **happy** frogs are a sign of a healthy, **happy** planet.

———————————◆———————————

*De todos nosotros depende asegurarnos de que las ranas tengan hábitats limpios y seguros donde puedan seguir creciendo. Las ranas saludables y **felices** indican un planeta saludable y **feliz**.*

Red-eyed tree frog
Rana verde de ojos rojos

Let's make the frogs **happy**.

*Hagamos **felices** a las ranas.*

Glossary • *Glosario*

amphibian – an animal that spends part of its life cycle in water and part of it on land; frogs, toads, and salamanders are amphibians

anfibio – un animal que pasa parte de su ciclo de vida en el agua y parte en la tierra; las ranas, los sapos y las salamandras son anfibios

camouflage – a way of hiding by blending into the surrounding environment or background

camuflaje – una forma de esconderse, confundiéndose con el entorno o el fondo

habitat – the natural home or environment where a plant or an animal lives

hábitat – el hogar o entorno natural donde vive una planta o un animal

life cycle – the series of changes in form and activity that a plant or an animal goes through during its life

ciclo de vida – la serie de cambios en la forma y la actividad de una planta o un animal a lo largo de su vida

pollution – harmful or poisonous substances in the air or water

contaminación – sustancias dañinas o venenosas en el aire o en el agua

predator – an animal that lives by killing and eating other animals

depredador – un animal que mata y come a otros animales para vivir